A boy, Karol Wojtyla, was born in 1920 in a small town in Poland. Years later he was to become known to millions of people all over the world as His Holiness Pope John Paul II. Here is his story.

Acknowledgments:
The author and publishers wish to acknowledge the use of photographs as follows: page 48 (bottom) J. Arthur Dixon, Newport; page 13, Fotocolor ENIT, Rome; pages 10, 29, 33 (top right and bottom), 38, 39, 43 (top), Tim Graham; pages 44/45 Christopher Hume, Camera Press; pages 11 (bottom), 32, 43 (bottom), 50 (bottom), Anwar Hussein; pages 11 (top), 34, 35 (top), Alan Hutchison Library; page 49 (top) Jarrold and Sons Ltd; page 30 and front and back endpapers, portrait studies by Karsh of Ottawa, Camera Press; page 22, Keystone Press; pages 4 (top), 6, 8, 9, 14 (bottom), 15, 18, 21, 33 (top left), 36, 41, 42, 48 (centre), 50 (top), 51, Camera Press, London; page 48 (top), Recreational Services Dept, Manchester; pages 48/49, Space Frontiers Ltd; pages 4 (bottom), 7, 14 (top), 26, 27, 31, 35 (bottom), 37, 40, 46, 47, Frank Spooner Pictures; pages 12, 25, 49 (bottom), Syndication International Ltd; and the Polish Embassy. Every effort has been made to trace copyright owners and any omissions will be added in the next edition.

First Edition

His Holiness

Pope John Paul II

written by JOAN COLLINS MA (Oxon)

Ladybird Books Loughborough

Black Smoke, White Smoke

Pope Paul VI

On 14th October 1978, a hundred and eleven Cardinals of the Roman Catholic Church met in the Sistine Chapel in the Vatican in Rome to choose a new Pope.

1978 was called 'The Year of Three Popes', because Pope Paul VI died on 6th August, and his successor, John Paul I, died suddenly in his sleep, thirty-three days after he had been appointed. Now a third Pope had to be chosen.

The Cardinals, in their splendid scarlet robes, sat facing each other in rows in the Sistine Chapel.

The inauguration of Pope John Paul I in August 1978. Cardinal Wojtyla knelt at the Pope's feet, little knowing that in thirty-three days, he himself would be the new Pope

The Cardinals gather in the Sistine Chapel for the election of the new Pope

There were Africans, Asians and Australians among them, as well as Europeans and Americans, for they came from all over the world. On the ceiling over their heads was the famous painting of the *Creation*, by Michelangelo, and on the wall above the altar, his scene of *The Last Judgment*. All the doors were locked and the telephone disconnected. They were shut in and could not come out till they had chosen their Pope.

The Pope is the head of the Roman Catholic Church, the successor to St Peter. When a Pope dies the Cardinals pray to God to direct their new choice.

Cardinal Wojtyla and his friend, the American Cardinal Baum, prepare for the meeting to elect the new Pope

In one corner of the Sistine Chapel, there is a stove with a chimney leading to the roof. A smoke signal is sent up from it, to tell the outside world what is happening. Bundles of chemical sticks lay ready to be burned in it, some making black smoke, some white. If the smoke from the chimney was black, nothing had been decided. If it was white, a new Pope had been named.

The eyes of the world were fixed on that chimney. The television cameras and crews were in St Peter's Square. There was even a spot-light trained on the chimney, in case the signal came at night. It was just after five o'clock, on the second day, that a puff of smoke was seen. It was greyish! Would it turn white or black?

Crowds came to St Peter's Square for two days to wait for this traditional signal that a new Pope has been elected

"Bianca! Bianca!" shouted the Italian crowd. It was white. Then a scarlet figure came out on a balcony, high up on the front of St Peter's, under the white dome. It was the Senior Cardinal.

"Habemus Papam!" he cried in Latin, the language of the Church. "We have a Pope!" Then, as the cheering died away, "He is Karol Wojtyla. He has chosen the name, John Paul II."

A gasp went up from the crowd. The choice was a great surprise. Karol Wojtyla was a Polish Archbishop from Krakow, the first non-Italian Pope for over four hundred years. He was unusually young, too: only fifty-eight. And he was a Pope from a Communist country behind the Iron Curtain.

The first non-Italian Pope since the 16th century makes his first public appearance as Pope John Paul II

"Warm, strong and joyful"

Then the Pope himself came out on the balcony. He was a sturdy, square-set man with a strong, kindly face. He spoke in a clear ringing voice, in Italian. "Your language — no, *our* language," he said. "You must forgive me if I make any mistakes." This delighted the Italian crowd.

There were not going to be any difficulties about understanding him. He could speak seven or eight languages. He amazed Bishops and journalists by the easy way he changed from one language to another as he spoke to people from different parts of the world.

The Pope had chosen his new name well. Everyone had loved the gentle Pope John Paul I, with his friendly smile. He had made the Pope seem a very human figure in his short time of office.

Pope John Paul II was full of energy and enthusiasm. He loved people and wanted to be with them, so it was not long before some of the traditions of the Vatican were changed. He began "travelling the pathways of the world", as he put it, to find out the needs of its people, instead of remaining inside the Vatican walls.

The leaders of the other World Churches were invited to his inauguration ceremony. Dr Coggan *(below)*, then Archbishop of Canterbury, described the Pope as a man who was "warm, strong and joyful", everything a Christian should be.

The City and the World

The Pope's Latin blessing, *Urbi et Orbi*, heard often on television, means 'to the City and to the World'. The City is Rome, because the Pope is the Bishop of Rome, but the whole world is his parish.

He lives in the Vatican, a city inside the city of Rome. It is the smallest independent State in the world. It has its own radio station, Radio Vatican, its own newspaper, stamps and money, and contains some of the most fabulous art treasures in the world. The Swiss Guards who patrol the gates wear colourful traditional uniforms.

St Peter's Church, which is one of the largest churches in the world, stands on the old site of the Emperor Nero's Roman Circus, where gladiators

Above: *The Swiss Guard dates back to the early 16th century and their uniform is said to have been designed by Michelangelo*

The Pope seen riding with the French President, Giscard d'Estaing, in one variety of Popemobile

Papal audience in the new audience hall at the Vatican

fought and Christians were thrown to the lions in the first century AD. St Peter's Square can hold as many as 300 000 people. Pilgrims come from all over the world to be blessed by the Pope, who gives audience to individuals and groups in his palace, and comes out into the Square on Wednesdays to meet the people. In the early days, he was driven around in his white jeep, now known as the *Popemobile*, and then took his place on a raised seat, from which he spoke to the crowd.

H M Queen Elizabeth II visited the Pope at the Vatican in 1980

The Square has a special meaning for the Pope. In earlier days he wrote a poem about it. Here are some lines from it.

Marble floor

Our feet meet the earth in this place;
there are so many walls, so many colonnades,
yet we are not lost. If we find
meaning and one-ness,
it is the floor that guides us...
Peter, you are the floor, that others
may walk over you... You guide their steps...
You want to serve their feet that pass
as rock serves the hooves of sheep.
The rock is a gigantic temple floor,
the cross a pasture.

St Peter's name means 'a rock' and Christ said of him, "On this Rock I will build my Church." The poem is really about the role of the Pope, who is a shepherd to his flock; a guide to the Church.

It may seem strange that a Pope can be also a poet but Pope John Paul II is a man of many unexpected talents and interests. He is also a daring, first-class skier, a lover of mountains and lakes, a climber, a swimmer and expert canoeist. He enjoys vigorous exercises and has even had an Olympic-style swimming pool installed at his summer home in Castel Gandolfo.

The Papal palace at Castel Gandolfo (above and below)

The Boy who grew up to be Pope

The Poles felt enormous pride when their Archbishop was made Pope. Great sadness was mixed with their joy, however, when the people realised that their Archbishop could never make his home in Poland again. One friend said, "I hope he will be able to get Polish mushrooms in the Vatican!" The Pope loves simple country food, and it is nice to know he has some Polish nuns to cook for him in his kitchen.

The Pope was born Karol Wojtyla, in 1920, in a small market town

Karol Wojtyla with his mother

called Wadowice. It is on the edge of the hills at the foot of the Tatra mountains, near the border with Czechoslovakia. He went to the local primary school and lived with his family in a small, ordinary apartment, without a bathroom. They were not 'well-off'. His father had been a soldier and had a small pension. Karol's mother died when he was only nine years old.

The Wojtyla family lived in this house in Wadowice

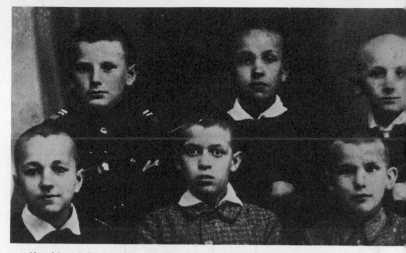

Karol (top left) *with his fellow pupils at the primary school in Wadowice*

Five years later his elder brother, Edward, a doctor, died of scarlet fever. This left Karol and his father alone and they became very close. His father was a man of strong religious faith, and Karol went to the church and served as an altar boy at Mass.

Lolek, as he was nicknamed (and is still called by his very oldest friends), was a bright boy. He was an all-rounder, popular, and a born leader, though he was younger than some of his friends. He played football, liked sports, especially ski-ing, and was good company. He was especially clever at learning languages.

When he was at school at Wadowice, he had been chosen to make a speech when the Archbishop of Krakow, Prince Sapieha, came on a visit. The Archbishop was so impressed that he asked the headmaster if the boy had ever thought of becoming a priest. "Not that I know of," the headmaster replied. "He wants to be an actor."

When he was eighteen, Karol and his father moved to Krakow. Karol went to the University there and became a student of Polish language and literature.

During his first year the times were troubled and World War II was approaching.

Tanks rumbled down the Polish streets and German soldiers occupied the towns, determined to break the Polish spirit and destroy Poland as a nation. They set up concentration camps, imprisoning all Jews and anyone who was likely to lead a resistance movement. Two of the worst camps, Auschwitz and Birkenau, were in the district where Karol lived.

The universities were closed and all the books burned in the streets. The teachers were sent away. Every student was in danger. They had to find other work quickly and to get labour permits or they would be sent to Germany to work in the slave gangs.

Karol and some of his friends found work as labourers in a stone quarry, breaking up rocks and loading them into overhead wagons.

The students helped the underground movement to hide Jewish families from the Nazis. They were also determined to go on with their own education in secret. They held meetings to read poetry and to act in plays by Polish writers, to keep the culture of their own people alive.

Karol was beginning to think seriously about becoming a priest. About this time his father died which was a great loss to him. He also had a serious accident, with head injuries. Although the University had been closed by the Nazis, it still ran courses in

The courtyard at Krakow University where Karol Wojtyla studied

secret. When he recovered, Karol knew he had a calling to be a priest and took the important step of enrolling at the University as a theological student. Karol Wojtyla worked in a chemical factory all day, and studied hard at night.

The same Archbishop, Prince Sapieha, who had heard Karol's speech at school, decided to hide his young student-priests in his palace, where the Germans would not search. Karol was in the palace, living in secret, for two long years.

When peace came it did not bring happiness, for Karol's part of Poland was 'liberated' by Stalin's Red Army. The students came out of hiding and started to rebuild their ravaged University. But the Soviet government did not encourage religion.

At this time a new life began for Karol. He was sent to Rome to study philosophy. It was the first time he had been outside Poland. Now he was in an ancient and marvellous city. He made the most of his opportunities, meeting new people and ideas, and practising his languages. In his vacations he worked for the Catholic War Relief Service. When Karol returned from Rome, he was given a small country parish at Niegowice, his first experience as *Father* Wojtyla, and a great change from his years of study.

The Priest in the shabby cassock

When we see pictures of Pope John Paul II in his splendid robes, it is difficult to imagine him as a young priest, trudging through the snow to visit distant farmhouses, in a shabby black cassock, its hem stiff with frozen mud. He never wore an overcoat. His parishioners gave him warmer clothes, but somehow he always found somebody who needed them more than he did.

The Pope (centre) was ordained as a priest in 1946 having completed his studies in Krakow

18

Father Wojtyla's first parish church at Niegowice

Karol Wojtyla never seemed to care about possessions or what he was wearing. (There is a story that, when he was made a Cardinal, he arrived in black socks, because he could not find any red ones!)

What he did care about was his people. They still remember his short time with them and, after he left, found excuses to invite him back to family celebrations, especially carol-singing in their homes at Christmas, which he loved.

He helped his parishioners to build a new church. This was one important way in which Christians could show their faith under Communist rule.

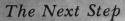

The Next Step

Father Wojtyla was soon transferred to the city churches — St Florian's and later St Catherine's, in Krakow. He went to the University of Lublin, the only Catholic University in the Communist world. There he became a professor, a post he still holds as Pope. He told his students they would have to come to the Vatican for classes!

He has always had a special relationship with students. He is not only a born teacher but shares and understands their interests, their love of singing, and their out-door activities. Father Wojtyla was the obvious choice for Student Chaplain. When he became a Bishop, he still made time for his students who called him 'Wujek' (little uncle).

20

A Bishop on a Bicycle

His progress in the Church was rapid. The parish priest of the church in Wadowice, where Karol was baptised, kept a proud record.

1st November 1946	Priest
28th September 1958	Bishop
30th December 1963	Archbishop of Krakow
26th June 1967	Cardinal

The last entry, 16th October 1978, was Pope.

He was only thirty-eight when he was made a Bishop. It did not change his life-style at all. True, instead of walking everywhere he had a bicycle, and even a rather ancient car and chauffeur to go round the diocese. He hated wasting time, so he had a table and a light fixed in the car, so that he could read and work on the journeys.

His appetite for work was amazing. There were not enough hours in the day for him, yet he never refused to see anybody who wanted to talk to him.

He was often late for meals and the soup would be cold, because someone had waylaid him.

When he became Pope, he found there was a tradition that the Pope always ate alone. That did not suit him at all. He used meals, as he always had, as a good way of meeting and talking to people.

Cardinal Wojtyla (centre) in 1974, visiting a village near Krakow

21

As Bishop, he had a lot of paper work, and so less time for his students, and for the outdoor exercise he found so essential. So he combined the two. He took his students on long mountaineering and walking expeditions, and taught them sitting round him on a hillside. Dressed in old trousers and jacket, he did not look like a Bishop at all.

When he moved into the Palace at Krakow he chose a small room with plain furniture, just a bed, table and two chairs, but he carried in a pair of skis over his shoulder and propped them against the wall.

There was another very important side to his nature. He drew his strength from prayer. He always set aside certain hours in the day when he was not to be interrupted, and spent them alone in private worship.

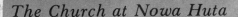

The Church at Nowa Huta

When he was Bishop and Archbishop of Krakow, one of the things he did that will be long remembered was to help his people to build a remarkable new church, in spite of opposition from the State.

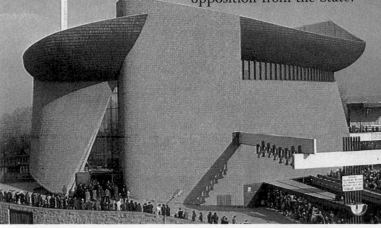

The Polish government built a new town for the workers at the Lenin Steel Plant. It was a showplace, at Nowa Huta, near Krakow. There was a huge statue of Lenin there, and concrete blocks of workers' flats, but no church.

The people asked permission to build a church, but were refused. Supported by their Bishop, they pressed for one so strongly that in 1967 the government gave way but would supply no money. It took ten years to raise this, but it was done, and a striking, unusual church was built. One of his last acts in the year before Archbishop Wojtyla became Pope was to dedicate this church.

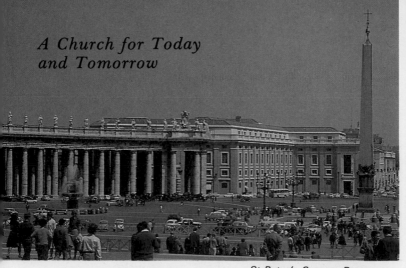

A Church for Today and Tomorrow

After the war, the Roman Catholic Church took a fresh look at some of its traditions and at the part it should play in the modern world.

The Popes were the leaders in the search for an answer. In 1962, Pope John XXIII, then old, but determined, called the special Vatican Council I to discuss how the church could stand up for human rights to freedom, justice and a fair share of the world's resources for everybody.

Karol Wojtyla had been made an Archbishop in 1963, and joined in the Rome discussions of Vatican Council II, under Pope Paul VI, with enthusiasm. He had first-hand experience of life behind the Iron Curtain and could talk about human rights as they affected his people. His clear thinking and his down-to-earth suggestions made a strong impression on his colleagues in the Council. Equally important was his gift for languages.

He soon became more widely known and was
invited to travel, visiting European countries,
the USA and Canada, Australia, New Zealand,
Indonesia and the Far East.

Bishop Wojtyla

After meeting African Bishops, he wrote:

My dear brother, it's you, an immense land I feel
where rivers dry up suddenly — and the sun
burns the body as the foundry burns ore.
I feel your thoughts like mine.

The World his Parish

As Pope John Paul II, Karol Wojtyla shows the same tireless energy he had as a young country priest, striding through the snow to distant farmhouses in Niegowice. The difference is that now he boards helicopters and flies in a Boeing 727 (named *Shepherd I*) to the distant corners of the earth.

Although many ordinary Catholics might not have heard of him before 16th October 1978, he soon became a familiar and well-loved world figure. His early training as an actor in voice and gesture help to make him a great performer on the world's stage. He is able to project the love he feels to the countries and people he visits.

The Pope at work inside the aircraft

He kneels down to kiss the earth always, directly he arrives. He picks up children in his arms, talks to the parents in a fatherly way, joins groups of students in songs, and blesses the old, the sick and the handicapped.

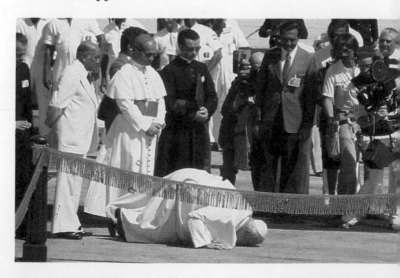

What the Pope wears

The Pope always wears a white buttoned cassock and skull-cap. He may wear a short red cape, and sometimes a long red cloak. Sometimes he wears a broad, flat red hat out of doors.

Priests wear similar garments in black, and cardinals wear red, or black cassocks with red buttons. They are given the special 'cardinal's hat' or *biretta* (square, red and pointed) by the Pope.

The Pope wears a band of white wool on his shoulders, like a yoke, with four purple crosses on it. This is to show he accepts the burden laid on him: to care for Christ's sheep. The wool is taken from two lambs which are brought to the altar of St Agnes' Church in Rome, while the *Agnus Dei* (O Lamb of God) is sung. The garment is called a *pallium* and is made by a special order of nuns. The Pope gives similar bands to Archbishops when they are elected.

He also wears a beautiful stole which has his coat of arms on it. Because of his special love for the Virgin Mary, it has the letter M and the picture of the Polish *Black Madonna* on it. There is also St Peter holding his keys to Heaven, and other symbols.

When the Pope celebrates Mass he sometimes wears a *mitre* on his head. He is often presented with mitres as gifts. They are usually beautifully ornamented with colours and symbols connected with the place he is visiting.

On his breast he wears the gold pectoral cross, and carries a straight *crosier* in his hand. (This is a staff with a crucifix at the top. Bishops carry hooked ones, like shepherds' crooks.)

The Pope wears a plain gold ring with his seal on it. This is the *Fisherman's Ring* (because St Peter was a fisherman) and it is always broken after the Pope's death.

He has other jewelled rings, usually with sapphires or amethysts. He gave one recently to the people in a slum area, just as Pope John Paul I had given some of his jewellery to help handicapped children.

The Pope's shoes are supposed to have red velvet on the outside, but Pope John Paul II prefers a more substantial covering.

All the Pope's vestments are made by the firm of Gamarelli, which has a shop near the Pantheon in Rome. They had made three sets in different sizes, to be ready for the election of a new Pope.

An unusual picture showing the Pope wearing a 'cowboy' hat in a motorcade in Guadalajara, Mexico

The Popemobile *drives through the crowd in Phoenix Park*

The Travelling Shepherd

The programme of the Pope's travels in his first two years of papacy is amazing.

January 1979	Mexico
June	Poland
September	Ireland, the USA and the United Nations in New York
November	Turkey
May-June 1980	Africa, France and Brazil

Wherever he went huge crowds thronged to meet him. In Mexico, ten million people lined the route when he drove from Mexico City to Puerta. He held open air masses in places like Phoenix Park, Dublin, and the Yankee Stadium in New York. When he held one in Krakow, nearly three-quarters of a million people attended.

The Pope loves to meet his people

Celebrating Mass

For each visit the Pope has a purpose and message. Although he meets statesmen and church dignitaries, he feels that his real mission is to the people, and in Third World countries — 'a pilgrimage to the poor'.

Latin America

In Mexico, the Latin-American churches were
holding a conference and here, as in Brazil in 1980,
the Pope's message (in Spanish) was to urge the
powerful and wealthy to search their consciences and
to treat their poorer brothers with justice and
generosity. He spoke of the human right to freedom,
though he advised priests to try to change the human
heart, rather than change political systems.

*The Pope addresses 200,000 students outside the sanctuary of
Notre Dame de Guadalupe in Mexico*

Former Auschwitz prisoners help with Mass

(Below) At the Execution Wall

Poland

The high point of his visits was bound to be the emotional return to Poland. It began with a Mass at Auschwitz. Former prisoners in their pyjama-like blue and white striped uniforms took part and the Pope knelt in prayer at the Execution Wall. The climax was the open-air Mass at Krakow with Cardinal Wyszinski.

The Pope had reunions with his student friends, who kept him until midnight with their songs. One was, *May you live a hundred years!* The Pope is reported to have said, "Do you really want the Pope to live a hundred years?"

"Yes!" they cried.

"You'd better let him get some sleep then!" replied the Pope.

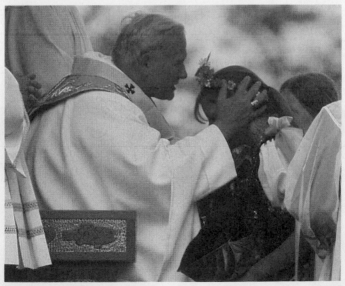

The Pope greets a young Polish girl in her national costume

Ireland

It really seemed as if the entire island came to Dublin to welcome the Pope, leaving the green countryside empty. He made a pilgrimage to the Marian shrine of Our Lady, at Knock. His message was about the importance of family life and spiritual values in a materialistic age. Then he flew from Shannon Airport, in *Shepherd I*, to the USA.

(Above and below) *Mass at Knock*

Leaving Shannon airport

The United States and UNO

In the United States, the Pope visited major cities and was entertained by President Carter *(below)* at the White House. His chief purpose was to make a strong plea for peace and human rights at the United Nations.

On his return to Europe he paid a courtesy visit to the Patriarch of the Orthodox Church, in Turkey.

Three countries in two months

On his second round of travels, the Pope spent seven days visiting six African countries, including Zaire, the Congo, Ghana, the Ivory Coast, Kenya and Upper Volta. He wanted to find out more about the new, young, African churches and the 'Africanisation' of the services, incorporating local languages and ethnic cultures.

Greeting Kenyan Bishops

In Zaire, the officiating Bishop wore a tribal head-dress instead of a mitre. There was traditional dancing, and spears were carried. For once the Pope did not know the languages, so could not join in. He spoke to them in French.

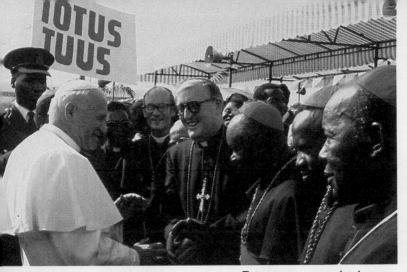

Totus tuus – *completely yours*

He found the Ghanaians very much like his own countrymen in their love of nature, joy in family life and the way they expressed these in poetry, song and dance.

42

In France the Pope addressed UNESCO and also workers in the St Denis communist quarter of Paris. He spoke of his belief in the dignity of human work, and asked them to think about the way in which men's technical skills were being used in the interests of greed, hatred and self-destruction. This recalls his poem,

The Armaments Factory Worker.

I cannot influence the fate of the globe.
Do I start wars? How can I know
whether I'm for or against?
No, I don't sin.
It worries me not to have influence,
that it is not I who sin.
I only turn screws, weld together
parts of destruction,
never grasping the whole,
or the human lot.

His last visit in 1980 was to Brazil, where he spent twelve crowded days, and reaffirmed more strongly his message of justice for the poor.

13th May 1981   How could they do it?

At 5.19 pm on Wednesday 13th May 1981, the world was shocked. St Peter's Square in the Vatican City was crowded with people who had come to Rome to see the Pope. The white dome of St Peter's Church stood out against the blue Italian sky.

The Pope's white jeep moved slowly among the crowds. He stopped to talk to people, to wave to children and to give his blessing. Suddenly shots were fired. The Pope crumpled and fell. Blood was seen on his white robes. The happy scene broke up in ugly confusion.

Guards seized a grim-faced young man, Mehemet Ali Acga, a Turkish terrorist, and snatched him out of the angry crowd. The jeep speeded up, through the Gate of Bells, into the Vatican, and moments later an ambulance took the Pope to the nearest hospital. He had been wounded in the arm and the stomach. The world saw this on television. Nobody could believe what had happened.

Christopher Hume, a student from New Zealand, unwittingly photographed the Pope's would-be assassin, seconds before he fired his pistol

"How could they do it?" the Pope said.

The assassin's motives have never been explained. He kept silent. Photographs show the Pope blessing a child and then collapsing.

The Pope instantly forgave his 'brother', as he called the unhappy young man. He saw his own suffering as a way of sharing world suffering.

He gradually recovered from two operations. His physical fitness and determination helped. He was supported by the prayers of the entire Christian world, not only Catholics. His sense of humour helped too. When he returned on 26th August 1981 to his regular Wednesday audiences the *Daily Telegraph* reported him as saying the equivalent of — "When I was so rudely interrupted..."

Africa 1982

As an indication that the Pope was fully recovered, he returned to Africa in February for a busy, four-nation tour. In eight days the Pope visited Nigeria, Benin, Equatorial Guinea and Gabon. He celebrated Mass with tens of thousands of people in the major cities and met leaders of non-Catholic Christian faiths and other religions.

The Pope was welcomed by all and he reaffirmed his message of two years before. He expressed hope and faith in the church's future in Africa and in the people of Africa.

Scenes from the Pope's visit to Nigeria

Whitsuntide 1982:
The Pope's Visit to Great Britain

In November 1981, plans for the Pope's visit went ahead. The Pope wanted to see as much of the British Isles and its people as possible, and to meet representatives of other churches as well as Catholics.

Liverpool Cathedral
Mass – Sunday 30th May

Heaton Park, Manchester
Mass – Monday 31st May

Westminster
Cathedral
Mass –
Friday 28th May

Pontcanna Fields, Cardiff
Young people's service
Wednesday 2nd June

Ninian Park Stadium, Cardiff
Mass – Wednesday 2nd June

Bellahouston Park, Glasgow
Mass — Tuesday 1st June

Murrayfield Stadium, Edinburgh
Mass — Monday 31st May

York — gathering
Monday 31st May

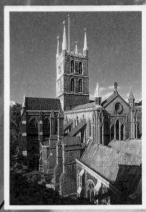

Southwark Cathedral
Service for the handicapped
Saturday 29th May

Coventry — Mass
Sunday 30th May

Wembley Stadium
Mass —
Saturday 29th May

Canterbury Cathedral
Ecumenical service
Saturday 29th May

49

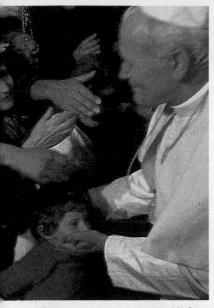

At the Vatican

In Kenya

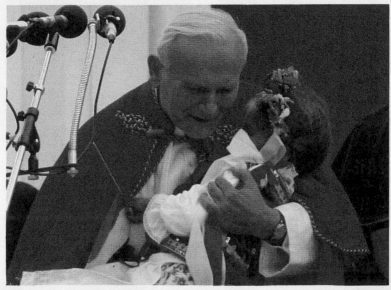

In Poland

The Pope and Children

In many photographs the Pope is seen with children, for whom he has a special feeling, expressed in these lines from a book of prayers he wrote for them. They show that his hope for the future relies on the rising generation.

In Japan

Our children!
You are the hope of the Pope!
You are called to be the bearers of generosity and honesty.

The Pope counts on you.
You are the strength and consolation of the Pope.